A Gift for

_____

From

_____

Date

_____

W9-COT-340

31 Days
with God

for Mothers

BARBOUR
PUBLISHING

© 2013 by Barbour Publishing, Inc.

Material taken and adapted from *Daily Wisdom for Mothers* by Michelle Medlock Adams.

Print ISBN 978-1-62416-883-3

eBook Editions:
Adobe Digital Edition (.epub) 978-1-63058-007-0
Kindle and MobiPocket Edition (.prc) 978-1-63058-008-7

All rights reserved. No part of this publication may be reproduced or transmitted for commercial purposes, except for brief quotations in printed reviews, without written permission of the publisher.

Churches and other noncommercial interests may reproduce portions of this book without the express written permission of Barbour Publishing, provided that the text does not exceed 500 words and that the text is not material quoted from another publisher. When reproducing text from this book, include the following credit line: "From *31 Days with God for Mothers*, published by Barbour Publishing, Inc. Used by permission."

All scripture quotations are taken from the King James Version of the Bible.

Published by Barbour Publishing, Inc., P.O. Box 719, Uhrichsville, Ohio 44683, www.barbourbooks.com

Our mission is to publish and distribute inspirational products offering exceptional value and biblical encouragement to the masses.

 Member of the
Evangelical Christian
Publishers Association

Printed in the United States of America.

Mom,
give God a month. . .
just see where He takes you!

*T*hese 31 easy-reading devotions provide help, hope, and a touch of humor for busy moms. Each day for an entire month, you'll be encouraged and energized by a meditation relating to a vital aspect of motherhood—peace, love, parenting, nurture, wisdom, knowledge, encouragement, and much more. Each reading will bring your thoughts back to the heavenly Father who cares so much about you, and the children you love.

Accompanied by inspiring prayers and quotations, practical tips, and lined space for recording your own thoughts, this book is the perfect way to celebrate the life God has called you to—the life of a loving mother.

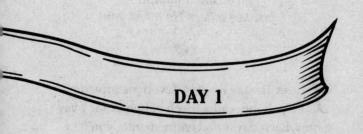

DAY 1

Time for a Break

Come unto me, all ye that
labour and are heavy laden,
and I will give you rest.

MATTHEW 11:28

$\mathcal{A}$hh. . .rest. Who wouldn't love a day of rest? But let's face it. Mothers don't really get a day of rest. If we rested, who would fix breakfast? Who would get the children ready for church? Who would do the laundry so your son can wear his lucky socks for the big game on Monday?

No, there's not a lot of rest in a mother's schedule. But that's not really the kind of rest Jesus is talking about in this verse. The rest mentioned here is the kind that only Jesus can provide. Resting in Jesus means feeling secure in Him and allowing His peace to fill your soul. That kind of rest is available to all—even mothers.

So, in the midst of the hustle and bustle of your life (even if you're elbow-deep in dishwater), you can rest in Him. Start by meditating on the Lord's promises and His everlasting love for you. Make a mental list of the things in your life that you are thankful for and praise God for each one. Allow His love to overwhelm you. . .and rest.

Mom to Master

Lord, help me to rest in You—
even when I'm overwhelmed with the
"To Do's" of each day. I want more of
You in my life. I love You. Amen.

If peace be in the heart, the wildest
winter storm is full of solemn beauty.

C. F. RICHARDSON

Think It Over

Do you take time to "rest" each day?

....
....
....
....
....

How would your life change if you focused on
God's promises during the most stressful part of
your day?

....
....
....
....
....

How would your resting in Christ affect your
family relationships?

....
....
....
....
....

It's the rests that make the
difference in the music of our lives.
They really are the pauses that refresh.

STEVE AND MARY FARRAR

Now the Lord of peace himself
give you peace always by all means.
The Lord be with you all.

2 THESSALONIANS 3:16

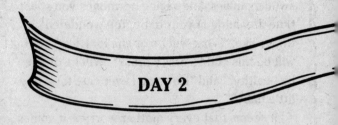

DAY 2

Worrywarts

*And Jesus answered and said
unto her, Martha, Martha, thou art
careful and troubled about many things:
But one thing is needful: and Mary
hath chosen that good part, which
shall not be taken away from her.*

LUKE 10:41–42

*D*o you remember when you were pregnant? In the midst of weird food cravings, swollen ankles, and raging hormones you spent time dreaming of your baby. You wondered things like: "What will he or she look like?" "What will be this child's first words?" "Will he or she be healthy?" and "How will I ever care for a tiny little baby?"

It seems that every mother worries. It comes so naturally. Most first-time moms worry that they won't be equipped with the appropriate parenting skills needed to be a good mom. Then the baby comes—and with it, a whole new set of worries. As the child grows, the worries grow, too. Sometimes, they can become almost suffocating.

When we feel overwhelmed with the worries that accompany motherhood, it means we've forgotten to figure God into the equation. With God, all things are possible—even raising good kids in a mixed-up world. God doesn't expect mothers to have all the answers, but He does expect us to go to Him for those answers. So, if worries are consuming your thoughts—go to God. He not only has the answers, He *is* the answer!

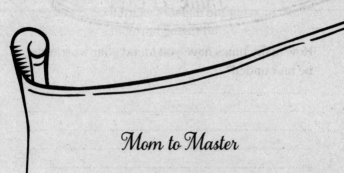

Mom to Master

God, I trust You with my children,
and I give You my worries. Amen.

Let the ways of childish confidence
and freedom from care. . .teach you what
should be your ways with God.

HANNAH WHITALL SMITH

Think It Over

How many times have you found your worries to be unfounded?

....

....

....

....

....

What message does your worrying send to your children?

....

....

....

....

....

How can you show them you have complete trust in God and His power?

....

....

....

....

....

Concern draws us to God.
Worry pulls us from him.

JOANNA WEAVER

Be careful for nothing; but in every
thing by prayer and supplication
with thanksgiving let your
requests be made known unto God.

PHILIPPIANS 4:6

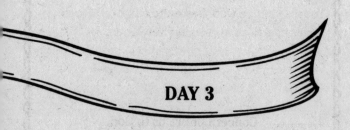

DAY 3

Unconditional Love

*Neither death, nor life, nor angels,
nor principalities, nor powers,
nor things present, nor things to come,
nor height, nor depth, nor any other
creature, shall be able to separate us
from the love of God, which is in
Christ Jesus our Lord.*

ROMANS 8:38–39

$\mathcal{S}$ome days it's harder to walk in love than others. Can I get an "Amen!" on that? On those days our love walk has quite a limp and we may find ourselves wondering how God can still love us. We'll think back over something we've said or done that was less than lovely, and our insides cringe.

This is especially true when it comes to our children. Of all the people in our lives, they are the ones to whom we want to show that unconditional, always-there-for-you kind of love. So when we fail to accomplish that goal, our heart hurts. But it's in those times that we sense the Father's presence in a big way. We can literally feel His love wrapping around us like a cozy sweater.

No matter how many times we fail, God still loves us. And, on those days when we know we're definitely not in the running for "Mother of the Year," that's good to know. God loves us even more than we love our children. In fact, the Word says that we're the apple of His eye. I like that. So, the next time your love walk becomes more of a crawl, remember—God adores you.

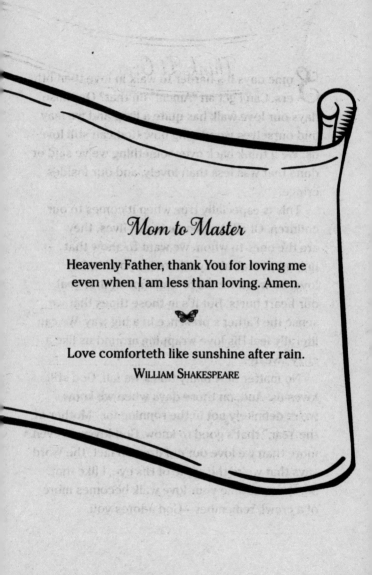

Mom to Master

Heavenly Father, thank You for loving me
even when I am less than loving. Amen.

Love comforteth like sunshine after rain.

WILLIAM SHAKESPEARE

Think It Over

Do you believe you are the apple of God's eye?

....
....
....
....
....

How can you embed in your heart the fact that God loves you—no matter what?

....
....
....
....
....

As you make God's love a reality for you, how will that change your life and that of your children?

....
....
....
....
....

Attentive love comes from God. He's the one who gives the ability to give and receive the right kind of love in all the right ways.

RHONDA REA

And the Lord make you to increase and abound in love one toward another, and toward all men, even as we do toward you.

1 THESSALONIANS 3:12

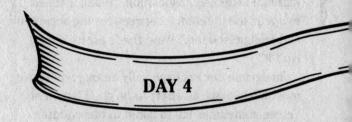

DAY 4

Earth to Mom. . .

A wise man will hear,
and will increase learning.
PROVERBS 1:5

$\mathcal{L}$ istening. It's almost a lost art form in today's world. Yet according to the International Listening Association, "Being listened to spells the difference between feeling accepted and feeling isolated." Wow, that's pretty strong, isn't it?

In certain circles, especially among adults, we most likely make an effort to be good listeners. Yet we sometimes fail to listen to our children. We find ourselves interrupting them, trying to get them to "get to the end of the story" while we're still somewhat young. We may even have the adage "Children should be seen and not heard" running through our head while our child pours his or her heart out to us. But that's not what we should be doing as caring, accepting moms.

Are you a good listener? Do you really give your kids your full attention when they are talking to you? Do you nod your head and smile, letting them know that you're truly into what they are saying? Are you present in the moment? If not, you may need to ask God to help you improve your listening skills. If we fail to listen to them now, we'll be sorry later when they no longer choose to tell us things. So go ahead. Open up your ears and your heart and listen to your children!

Mom to Master

Lord, please help me to listen to my children
the same way that You listen to me. Amen.

The first duty of love is to listen.

PAUL TILLICH

Think It Over

In what ways, if any, do your listening skills need improvement?

....
....
....
....

How will knowing that listening—not speaking—is the most important aspect of communication change the way you converse with your child and with God?

....
....
....
....

How can you let your child know you hear what he or she is saying—or not saying, through body language, energy, and intonation?

....
....
....
....

Listening opens up another's spirit.
DRS. LES AND LESLIE PARROTT III

Wherefore, my beloved brethren,
let every man be swift to hear, slow to speak.
JAMES 1:19

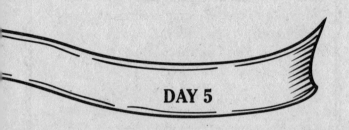

DAY 5

Stopping to Pray

*But thou, when thou prayest, enter into thy
closet, and when thou hast shut thy door,
pray to thy Father which is in secret.*

MATTHEW 6:6

$\mathcal{D}$o you have a sort-of bedtime ritual with your children? Some parents read a storybook to their children every night. Other parents share a Bible story or two. Some even make up their own stories to share. Whatever your bedtime routine might be, hopefully prayer is part of it.

Saying a bedtime prayer with your children is one of the most important things you can do for them. It accomplishes several things, such as teaching your kids to pray by hearing you pray aloud, giving prayer a place of importance in their lives, making prayer a habit for them, drawing the family unit closer, and enriching their spiritual side. To put it in the words of my daughter Allyson, "Prayer rocks!"

We spend so much time just doing "stuff" with our kids—running them to soccer practice, helping with homework, playing board games— and all of that is good. But if we don't figure prayer time into the daily equation, we're just spinning our wheels. Prayer time is a precious time. Don't miss out on it even one night. It's a habit worth forming!

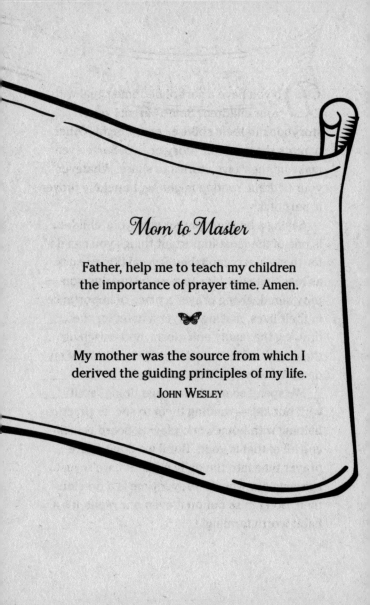

Mom to Master

Father, help me to teach my children
the importance of prayer time. Amen.

My mother was the source from which I
derived the guiding principles of my life.
JOHN WESLEY

Think It Over

What can you do to let your child know you
make prayer a part of your daily routine?

....

....

....

....

How can you find a way to show your child that
God does answer prayer?

....

....

....

....

How can you demonstrate that prayers should
come from the heart?

....

....

....

....

....

Prayer is a declaration of our dependence on God. It isn't something mechanical you do; it is somewhere you go to meet Someone you know.

JILL BRISCOE

Yet the LORD will command his lovingkindness in the daytime, and in the night his song shall be with me, and my prayer unto the God of my life.

PSALM 42:8

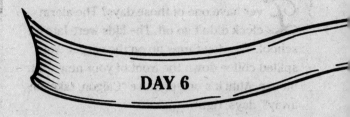

DAY 6

A No Good, Very Bad Day

Casting all your care upon him;
for he careth for you.

1 PETER 5:7

$\mathcal{E}$ ver have one of those days? The alarm clock didn't go off. The kids were late for school. The dog threw up on the carpet. You spilled coffee down the front of your new white blouse. Ahh! It's one of those "Calgon, take me away!" days, right?

But it doesn't have to be. No matter how many challenges you face today, you can smile in the face of aggravation. How? By casting your cares upon the Lord. That's what the Lord tells us to do in His Word, yet many of us feel compelled to take all of the cares upon ourselves. After all, we're mothers. We're fixers. We're the doers of the bunch. We wear five or six fedoras at a time—we can handle anything that comes our way, right?

Wrong! But God can. When the day starts to go south, cast your cares on Him. He *wants* you to! As mothers, we can handle a lot, but it's true what they say—Father really does know best. So, give it to God. C'mon, you know you want to.

Mom to Master

Lord, help me to turn to You when my
troubles seem too big to face alone and
even when they don't. Help me to trust
You with all of my cares. Amen.

Thou art coming to a King
Large petitions with thee bring;
For His grace and power are such
None can ever ask too much.

JOHN NEWTON

Think It Over

How do you cast your cares on God—by counting blessings, breathing deeply, belting out praises, etc.?

....

....

....

....

....

Do you find your kids following your example when they face stressful situations?

....

....

....

....

....

How can you help yourself—and your children—cast *every* care upon the One meant to carry them?

....

....

....

....

....

If you feel that the weight of your circumstances is too heavy to bear, maybe it's because the burden is yours, not His.

<small>JENNIFER ROTHSCHILD</small>

Ye have seen what I did unto the Egyptians, and how I bare you on eagles' wings, and brought you unto myself.

<small>EXODUS 19:4</small>

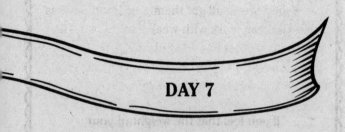

DAY 7

Wonderful Weaknesses

And he said unto me, My grace is sufficient for thee: for my strength is made perfect in weakness. Most gladly therefore will I rather glory in my infirmities, that the power of Christ may rest upon me.

2 CORINTHIANS 12:9

Nobody likes to admit weaknesses but, hey, we've all got them. The good news is this—God can work with weakness. In fact, His Word tells us that His power is made perfect in our weakness. Pretty cool, eh? So, why is it so difficult to admit we have weaknesses?

Let's be honest. Most of us hate to admit—especially to our children—that we have weaknesses. We want to appear perfect and "superhero-like," to think our kids have got the coolest mom in the world—a mom who loves God, loves them, and can still skateboard with the best of them. But over the past few years, our children have probably figured out that Mom has got some weaknesses—definitely! The cat is out of the bag, so to speak.

And we should be okay with that. If we let our children see our shortcomings, they'll feel better about their own weaknesses. So quit trying to disguise your weaknesses or make excuses for them. Just admit you've got them and let God's power be made perfect in them.

Mom to Master

Father, thank You for working
through my weaknesses. Amen.

As a countenance is made beautiful by
the soul's shining through it, so the world
is beautiful by the shining through it of God.

FRIEDRICH HEINRICH JACOBI

Think It Over

How do you try to disguise your weaknesses?

....
....
....
....
....

What weaknesses do you have that you also see in your children?

....
....
....
....
....

How can you and your children—together— admit to and work through your weaknesses?

....
....
....
....
....

There is strength in being weak—God's strength!
Let God step in and do what you cannot.

BARB ALBERT

*[God] giveth power to the faint; and to them
that have no might he increaseth strength.*

ISAIAH 40:29

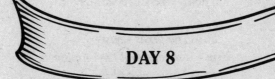

DAY 8

Thanksgiving Isn't Just for November

My brethren, count it all joy when ye fall into divers temptations.

JAMES 1:2

I recently visited a website that made me feel a bit guilty for all the times that I've complained about everyday stuff. Its headline said:

THINGS TO BE THANKFUL FOR

The taxes I pay—
because it means that I'm employed.
The clothes that fit snugly—
because it means I have enough to eat.
The mounds of laundry—
because it means I have clothes to wear.

Okay, let's be honest. Have we ever been thankful for taxes, extra weight, or loads of laundry? Probably not. But it is an interesting concept. We should be looking for reasons to be thankful—even in the stuff that would not ordinarily fill our hearts with gratitude.

And we should impart that same attitude of gratitude into our kids. So when your daughter doesn't get invited to "the big party," she can be thankful that she has a mom who will take her to the movies instead. Or when your son doesn't make the football team, he can be thankful that he has more free time to practice his guitar. It's really about looking for that silver lining in every gray cloud. Find that silver lining today.

Mom to Master

Lord, I praise You for the good and
not-so-good things in my life. Amen.

Throughout life we hardly realize that
we receive a great deal more than we give.
It is only with gratitude that life becomes rich.

<small>DIETRICH BONHOEFFER</small>

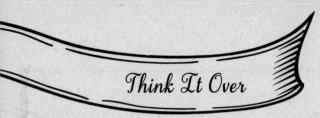

Think It Over

How do you express your gratitude to God for
the good *and* the not-so-good?

....

....

....

....

....

How often do you tell your children that you are
thankful for them?

....

....

....

....

....

How do you feel about the not-so-good things
after you've counted your blessings?

....

....

....

....

....

We can thank God for everything good,
and all the rest we don't comprehend yet.

KRISTIN ARMSTRONG

*In every thing give thanks: for this is the
will of God in Christ Jesus concerning you.*

1 THESSALONIANS 5:18

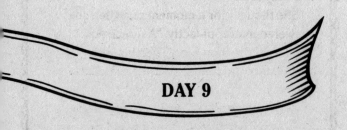

DAY 9

Movie-Star Dreams

*I can do all things through Christ
which strengtheneth me.*

PHILIPPIANS 4:13

What do you want to be when you grow up?" I asked my daughter Ally when she was only four.

She thought for a moment and then she answered matter-of-factly, "A movie star."

"Great," I responded. "Then you can pay for Mommy and Daddy's retirement condo in Florida."

Children know how to dream big. Do you know why? Because no one has told them yet that they can't. That's what we love about kids. They don't have that inner voice that says, *You can't be a movie star. You're not good enough. You're not pretty enough. You'll never be able to accomplish your dream.* No, they believe they can do anything. And you know what? They're right! God's Word says that we can do all things through Christ who gives us strength. All means all, right?

That's why Jesus said we should have childlike faith. We should be able to believe big when it comes to the dreams and ambitions that God has placed within us. God wouldn't have placed them there if He weren't going to help us achieve them. So learn from your kids. Get back that childlike faith and start believing.

Mom to Master

Lord, help me to believe You like
my children believe You. Help me
to dream big like they do. Amen.

Far away, there in the sunshine,
are my highest aspirations. . . . I can
look up and see their beauty, believe in
them, and try to follow where they lead.

LOUISA MAY ALCOTT

Think It Over

What dreams did you have as a child?

....
....
....
....
....

What dreams do you have now?

....
....
....
....
....

After applying your faith, what steps can you take to make your dream(s) a reality?

....
....
....
....
....

I want you to be encouraged that in God's time you will see the dreams and visions that God has given you fulfilled.

JOYCE MEYER

Now unto him that is able to do exceeding abundantly above all that we ask or think, according to the power that worketh in us, unto him be glory in the church by Christ Jesus throughout all ages, world without end. Amen.

EPHESIANS 3:20–21

DAY 10

Your B.F.F. (Best Friend Forever)

Trust in the name of the Lord,
and stay upon. . .God.
ISAIAH 50:10

*D*o you remember that song "Lean on Me" by Al Green? Club Nouveau remade it back in the '80s. The words to that song are rather inspirational in nature. Do you remember them? "Lean on me. When you're not strong, I'll be your friend. I'll help you carry on." (You're singing along right now, aren't you?)

If there's anything moms need, it's someone to lean on from time to time. When the dishwasher is broken, the car is in the shop, the kids are sick, the bank account is empty, and payday is a week away. . .we all need somebody to lean on.

We can be so thankful that we have God to lean on during difficult times. Even if our family or friends don't understand our feelings and even if there's no one else to lean on, we've always got God. He promises in His Word to never leave us nor forsake us. We can lean on Him, and He's happy to let us. So, if you're having a lousy day, a lousy week, or even a lousy year, God understands and He loves you. Go ahead— lean on Him. He will be your Friend. He'll help you go on.

Mom to Master

Thank You, Lord, that I can lean on You.
Thanks for always being there for me. Amen.

When you have accomplished your daily tasks,
go to sleep in peace. God is awake.

VICTOR HUGO

Think It Over

To whom or what do you run when things go
wrong?

....

....

....

....

....

What stops you from running to God and handing
your difficulties over to Him?

....

....

....

....

....

What promises of God can you rely on to get you
through tough times?

....

....

....

....

....

When your friends and loved ones fail you,
God remains by your side, steadfast and true.

LIZ CURTIS HIGGS

*The LORD searcheth all hearts, and understandeth
all the imaginations of the thoughts: if thou
seek him, he will be found of thee.*

1 CHRONICLES 28:9

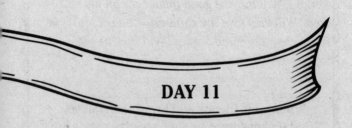

DAY 11

Under the Influence

Little children, let no man deceive you.
1 JOHN 3:7

*D*o you ever worry about the friends that your children are making? Do you often wonder, *Will they be good influences on my children? Will they hurt my children? Do they know Jesus as their Lord and Savior? Will they be lifelong, trustworthy friends?*

While we don't know the answers to all of these questions, we do know one thing—Jesus will be their lifelong Friend. They will always be able to count on Him. He will come through for them time and time again. He will stand by them no matter what. How do we know these things? Because He's been there for us when nobody else was.

We discover early in life that friends sometimes let us down—even our best friends—because they're human. If we put our hope in friends, disappointment and hurt are inevitable. But God is a sure thing.

We may realize that we can't pick our children's friends, and we know that we can't protect them from the hurt that comes from broken friendships and disloyalty. But there are two things we *can* do—we can teach them about Jesus, and we can pray that the Lord sends them godly companions. And we can start today.

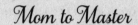

Mom to Master

Lord, please send my children good friends.
I'm thankful that You're their best
friend and mine. Amen.

Beneath God's watchful eye
His saints securely dwell;
That hand which bears all nature up
Shall guard His children well.

WILLIAM COWPER

Think It Over

What do you consider to be the qualities of a good friend?

....
....
....
....
....

In what ways can you show your children that Jesus is *your* best friend?

....
....
....
....
....

How can you help your children understand that Jesus wants them to always come to Him—no matter what they may have done?

....
....
....
....
....

Sometimes we might not even be aware
of the loving sacrifices a friend is making
on our behalf. That's what was so awesome
about Jesus' sacrifice: He gave His life
to save those who didn't know Him or
who rejected Him as their friend.

G. A. MYERS

*Greater love hath no man than this,
that a man lay down his life for his friends.*

JOHN 15:13

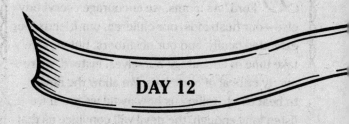

DAY 12

It's Your Turn!

*And the people the men of Israel
encouraged themselves.*
JUDGES 20:22

*D*o you ever encourage yourself in the Lord? As moms, we encourage everybody else—our husbands, our children, our friends, our extended family, and our neighbors. But we rarely take time to encourage ourselves. Instead, we're overly critical of ourselves. We allow the devil to beat us up, telling us how awful we are. If we listen long enough, the devil will convince us that we're unworthy to be servants of God. He'll tell us that we're horrible parents and wives. He'll tell us that we're failures in life. The devil will serve us condemnation with a side of guilt as often as we'll let him. It's time to tell him, *"No more!"*

We have to stop allowing the devil to deceive us. Don't dwell on his lies; instead, meditate on God's Word. The Bible says that you are fully able to fulfill your destiny. It says that no weapon formed against you is going to prosper. It says that you can do everything through God's strength. Stop focusing on what you can't do and start focusing on what you can do. Quit looking at how far you've got to go, and start looking at how far you've already come. Encourage yourself in the Lord today! It's your turn.

Mom to Master

Thank You, Lord, for giving me
the ability to fulfill my destiny.
Help me to stay encouraged. Amen.

You are special. God made you.
His undeserved love makes you somebody!

Alma Kern

Think It Over

In what ways do the devil's lies limit you?

....
....
....
....
....

In what ways do God's truths empower you?

....
....
....
....
....

What scriptures will you memorize to change
your negative thoughts into positive ones?

....
....
....
....
....

Satan's goal is to deafen us to God's voice
so that we embrace his thinking as easily
and naturally as if it were God's very own.

SHELLY BEACH

*When he [the devil] speaketh a lie,
he speaketh of his own: for he
is a liar, and the father of it.*

JOHN 8:44

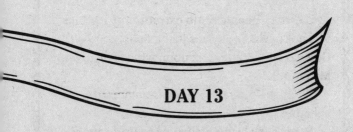

DAY 13

Extraordinary Requirements

*And I say also unto thee, That thou art Peter,
and upon this rock I will build my church;
and the gates of hell shall not prevail against it.*

MATTHEW 16:18

*D*id you know that God loves to use ordinary people to do extraordinary things?

Look at Peter. He was just a fisherman, but God called him the rock upon which "I will build My church."

What about Mary? She was an unmarried teenager, but God chose her to give birth to Jesus.

How about David? He was the little guy in the family. When his brothers went to war, he had to stay at home and watch over the sheep. Still, God called him to defeat the giant. Amazing, isn't it?

If you're feeling like you're not cut out for this motherhood job, cheer up! God is using you to do extraordinary things for His kingdom, too. He wouldn't have entrusted you with your precious children if He didn't believe you could handle it. Of course, it's difficult some days. But, hey, God is a big God—bigger than all of our doubts, transgressions, and faults. You don't have to be perfect. You just have to be available. Open your heart and let God restore your hope today. He has more extraordinary things in store for you!

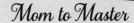

Mom to Master

Lord, do the extraordinary in
me and through me today. Amen.

The shocking message of the Bible continues
to be that God has chosen the least suspecting
of all vessels to do his greatest work. What you
are at this particular moment in your life is
irrelevant—your nationality, your education,
your personality. . . . What counts most is what
and who you are willing to become.

Tim Hansel

Think It Over

What and who are you willing to become?

....
....
....
....
....

What is holding you back from being extra-ordinary?

....
....
....
....
....

What can you do to tap in to God's power to be and do all He has created you to be and do?

....
....
....
....
....

God accomplishes extraordinary things through ordinary people who believe God can and will use them—imperfections and all.

DONNA PARTOW

We are his workmanship, created in Christ Jesus unto good works, which God hath before ordained that we should walk in them.

EPHESIANS 2:10

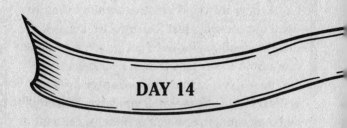

DAY 14

Getting Rid of the Grouchies

[Love] is not easily provoked.
1 CORINTHIANS 13:5

How is your attitude today? Feeling kind of grouchy? There are mornings that we open our eyes and just feel grouchy. It's as if the devil was waiting for us to get up so he could use our mouth to say ugly things. Ever been there? On those days, we have to force ourselves to walk in love. Let's face it. If you haven't been sleeping enough, or if you're under quite a bit of stress, or if you're feeling ill, it's easier to be a grouch.

But moms aren't supposed to be grouches! Haven't you ever seen *Leave It to Beaver* on TV Land? Mrs. Cleaver is always joyful. And how about that Carol Brady on *The Brady Bunch*? She is so sweet it's sickening!

In reality, no mom can be perfect all the time. We all lose our tempers. We all complain. We all act ugly. We all get grouchy. But God knew that when He created us. He knew our flesh would win out once in a while. That's why He sent Jesus to save us from our sins, so we can repent for our grouchy attitudes and move forward in love. So get those grouchies off and let love control you today.

Mom to Master

Lord, flood me with Your love. Amen.

For every minute you are angry,
you lose sixty seconds of happiness.

UNKNOWN

Think It Over

What things or people "push your buttons"?

....

....

....

....

....

In what ways can you rid your mind of the long-playing records of wrongs and replace them with unconditional love for others?

....

....

....

....

....

What can you do to make sure you get out of the right side of bed each morning?

....

....

....

....

....

Neither God nor our children expect us to be
perfect. But we can become examples of men
and women who genuinely love God and seek
to follow Him with a whole and earnest heart.

GIGI GRAHAM TCHIVIDJIAN

And now abideth faith, hope, charity,
these three; but the greatest of these is charity.

1 CORINTHIANS 13:13

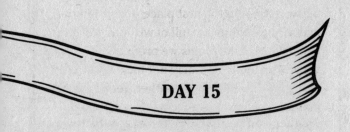

DAY 15

Wise Up!

*A word fitly spoken is like apples
of gold in pictures of silver.*

PROVERBS 25:11

It's funny—as young children we thought our moms knew everything. As teens, we thought they knew nothing. As adults, we realize we were right in the first place—they *do* know everything. Moms are full of wisdom; however, when we became moms we probably didn't feel very wise. In fact, we may not have known the first thing about being a mother. Yet as we've matured, we have learned a little about being a mom—most likely from our *own* moms. Their advice is priceless.

We can learn much from the godly women in our lives. Maybe your mom hasn't been there for you but God has placed other women in your life—an aunt, a grandmother, a close family friend, or your pastor's wife. Cherish their words of wisdom. God has placed them in your life for a purpose.

Just think, someday your children will look to you for wisdom—it's true! The Word says that they will rise up and call you blessed (see Proverbs 31:28). So make sure you have some wisdom to share. Treasure the advice that's been given to you and, more importantly, meditate on the Word of God. There's much wisdom waiting for you!

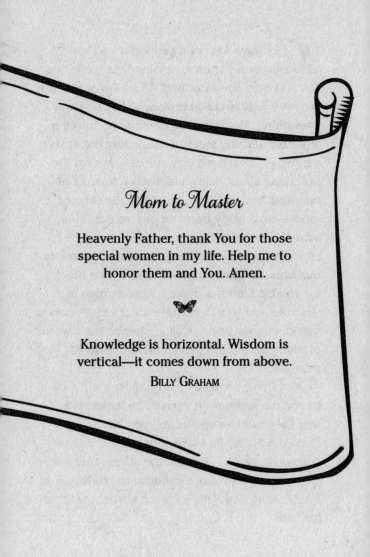

Mom to Master

Heavenly Father, thank You for those special women in my life. Help me to honor them and You. Amen.

Knowledge is horizontal. Wisdom is vertical—it comes down from above.

BILLY GRAHAM

Think It Over

What's the difference between knowledge and wisdom?

....
....
....
....
....

From whom have you gleaned most of your motherly wisdom?

....
....
....
....
....

How can you be assured that the advice you receive is in line with God's wisdom?

....
....
....
....
....

Being wise and being knowledgeable are two different things. But when knowledge begins with an understanding of God's character, our wisdom will continue to grow by merely acting on what we know.

VICKI KUYPER

Incline thine ear unto wisdom,
and apply thine heart to understanding.

PROVERB 2:2

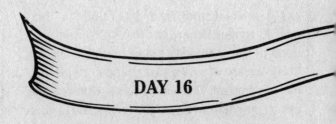

DAY 16

Supernatural Accountability

*Can the fig tree, my brethren, bear olive
berries? either a vine, figs? so can no
fountain both yield salt water and fresh.*

JAMES 3:12

We know from the Word of God that the tongue is hard to tame. Of course, we don't need the Bible to tell us that fact. Most likely, we are all well aware that our mouth is hard to control. That's why this scripture really brings conviction. If you're praising the Lord in church and hollering at your children on the way home, this scripture probably hits home.

We need to continually ask the Lord to put a watch on our mouths. We need to ask for His help so that we might be good examples for our children. If they see us praising God one minute and hollering at them the next, they will be confused and disillusioned with the things of God.

James 3:9 says, with the tongue "bless we God, even the Father; and therewith curse we men, which are made after the similitude of God." We must be careful of what we say because not only are our children listening, God is also listening. And we'll be held accountable for our words—all of them.

Mom to Master

Lord, please put a watch on my mouth that I might only speak good things. Help me to be a good example for my children. I love You. Amen.

Live so that your [children] will have a role model within arm's reach at all times.

VICKIE PHELPS

Think It Over

Which of your words do you sometimes hear coming out of your child's mouth?

....

....

....

....

....

What can you do to become more conscious of the words you say?

....

....

....

....

....

How can you reframe your words so that they come from a place of encouragement—not of discouragement?

....

....

....

....

....

A parent's voice is a megaphone
straight to the heart of a child.

BILL GLASS

For a child to be appropriately molded, parents
need to look at the model they're displaying
before their children. Children mimic well.

MAXINE MARSOLINI

Let no corrupt communication proceed out of your
mouth, but that which is good to the use of edifying,
that it may minister grace unto the hearers.

EPHESIANS 4:29

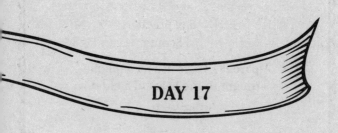

DAY 17

Taxi Time-Out

*Cast thy burden upon the LORD,
and he shall sustain thee: he shall
never suffer the righteous to be moved.*

PSALM 55:22

There are days when I'm sure the side of my SUV must say TAXI. We run to gymnastics. We race to cheerleading practice. We rush to art class. We hurry to Girl Scouts. We eat fast food on the way to computer class.

I want to stand up and say, "Stop the world from spinning! I want to get off!"

There is such pressure these days to make sure our children are in every extracurricular activity that sometimes I wonder if it's all too much. Have you been wondering the same thing?

We're moms. It's only natural that we desire to give our children the best. So it's no wonder we sign them up for all of these wonderful extracurricular opportunities. But be careful. Make sure you're not pushing and nudging your children right into burnout. We don't want our kids to be so overwhelmed with activities that they have no time to be kids. They only get one childhood. Ask God to help you enhance their growing-up years without overwhelming them with "stuff." Even good stuff, if there's too much of it, can be bad.

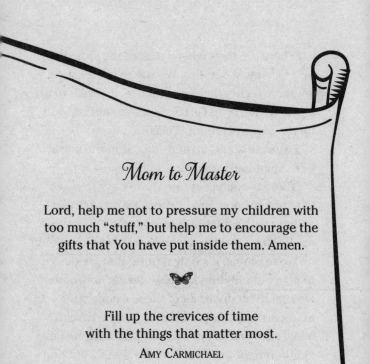

Mom to Master

Lord, help me not to pressure my children with too much "stuff," but help me to encourage the gifts that You have put inside them. Amen.

Fill up the crevices of time
with the things that matter most.

Amy Carmichael

Think It Over

In what ways does your child spend more time doing than being?

....
....
....
....
....

How does your child feel on days when he or she is rushing from one activity to another?

....
....
....
....
....

What changes can you make to your child's schedule to ensure he or she is living a more balanced life?

....
....
....
....
....

When we live life in a hurry,
we end up weary. . .in a hurry.

KERI WYATT KENT

In all thy ways acknowledge him,
and he shall direct thy paths.

PROVERBS 3:6

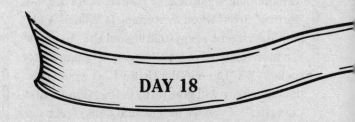

DAY 18

Gimme-ville

*Seek ye first the kingdom of God,
and his righteousness; and all these
things shall be added unto you.*

MATTHEW 6:33

*D*o your kids ever get the "Gimme Syndrome"? You know, the "Gimme this" and "Gimme that" disorder.. Of course, there are the "terrible twos" when everything is "Mine!" And then the tweens seem to bring out the "Gimmes" in a more expensive way. Instead of "Gimme that sucker," it's "Gimme that Go-Kart." (I wonder if the teen years will give birth to the "Gimme that Corvette!") Even we moms (and dads) feel a case of the Gimmes coming on at times. Not many in our society are immune.

No matter the season, the "Gimme Syndrome" is bad. You see, "Gimmes" always lead to more "Gimmes." The Bible might say it like this: "Gimmes beget gimmes." Once you fulfill the first "Gimme requests," there are always more to follow. It's continual!

But if we seek God first, all of our wants and "Gimmes" will be fulfilled. We need to keep our "Gimmes" under control and focus our energies on seeking God. If we breed little "Gimme" kids, they'll carry that mentality over into their relationship with God. Their prayers will be filled with, "Hi God. Gimme this and Gimme that. Amen." Ask God to get the "Gimmes" out of your household today. That's one request He'll be happy to fulfill!

Mom to Master

Lord, I pray that You remove the "Gimme Syndrome" from my household. Amen.

Thou hast given so much to me,
Give one thing more—a grateful heart;
Not thankful when it pleaseth me,
As if Thy blessings had spare days,
But such a heart whose pulse
may be Thy praise.

GEORGE HERBERT

Think It Over

What steps can you take to immunize your family from the must-have-now mentality?

....
....
....
....
....

In what ways can you help your child (and yourself) differentiate between "want" and "need"?

....
....
....
....
....

How can your child personally experience the idea that it really *is* more wonderful to give than to get?

....
....
....
....
....

It would be wonderful if we could stop accumulating so much stuff and start putting some of it to eternal use. The secret is keeping our worldly goods in spiritual perspective and maintaining a healthy balance.

JILL BRISCOE

I have shewed you all things, how that so labouring ye ought to support the weak, and to remember the words of the Lord Jesus, how he said, It is more blessed to give than to receive.

ACTS 20:35

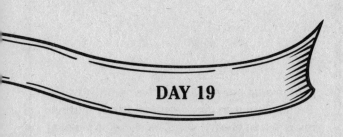

DAY 19

By the Grace of God

And by their prayer for you, which long after you for the exceeding grace of God in you. Thanks be unto God for his unspeakable gift.

2 CORINTHIANS 9:14–15

*G*race. We say grace. We name baby girls Grace. But do we really understand how wonderful God's grace is in our lives? Would you want to live one second without it operating in your life? *Grace* is defined as "God's unmerited favor." In other words, we didn't earn it. We certainly didn't deserve it, but God gave us His grace anyway. How great is that? And where you find grace, you almost always find mercy alongside it. Whew! That's good news, isn't it?

People who lived under the Law didn't have the luxury of grace. When they broke even the smallest rule, they were in a lot of trouble. But thank God we have His grace, because like any human, we mess up on a regular basis. But when we do mess up, we can run to Him. We don't have to hide, because when we repent, He gives us grace. He says, "That's okay, you'll do better next time."

In the same manner that God shows us grace, we should show our children grace. They aren't perfect, either. They are going to mess up once in a while. But if we show them grace, they won't hide from us when they get into trouble. Instead, they'll run straight into our arms.

Mom to Master

Father, I praise You for
the gift of grace. Amen.

Your worst days are never so bad that
you are beyond the reach of God's grace.
And your best days are never so good that
you are beyond the need of God's grace.

JERRY BRIDGES

Think It Over

What does *grace* mean to you?

....
....
....
....
....

In what situations do you find yourself grace-less?

....
....
....
....
....

What can you do to incorporate more grace into your life?

....
....
....
....
....

When a believer has been steeped in grace,
all the members of his or her immediate
society detect a refreshing fragrance.

CHRISTINE WOOD

*Grace and peace be multiplied unto you through
the knowledge of God, and of Jesus our Lord.*

2 PETER 1:2

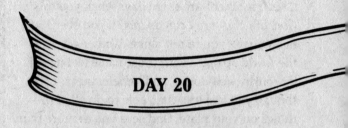

DAY 20

You Want Me?

And he [Gideon] said unto him,
Oh my Lord, wherewith shall I save Israel?
behold, my family is poor in Manasseh,
and I am the least in my father's house.

JUDGES 6:15

*D*o you ever feel incapable of being a good mother? Are there days when you think, *God, are You sure I can do this?* If you ever feel inadequate, you're not alone. Women all over the world struggle with those same feelings of insecurity, self-doubt, and hopelessness. Even though you feel less than able to do all of the things on your plate, God sees you as more than able to do everything He has called you to do.

Even great leaders in the Bible felt inadequate at times. Remember Moses' response when God called him to tell Pharaoh to let the Israelites go? Moses said that he couldn't possibly do it. He told God that He had the wrong guy before finally agreeing to do it. And what about Gideon? When God called him to lead His people against Midian, he said, "My family is poor in Manasseh, and I am the least in my father's house." Still, God addressed him as a "mighty man of valour" (Judges 6:12). See, God didn't see Gideon as a weak worm of the dust. He saw Gideon as a mighty man of valor. God sees you as mighty and strong and capable, too! Ask God to help you see yourself as He sees you.

Mom to Master

Lord, help me to see myself through
Your eyes. I love You. Amen.

The same God who guides the stars in their
courses, who directs the earth in its orbit,
who feeds the burning furnace of the sun and keeps
the stars perpetually burning with their fires—
the same God has promised to supply thy strength.

CHARLES SPURGEON

Think It Over

In what areas do you feel discouragement?

....

....

....

....

....

What Bible verses can you memorize to change
feelings of hopelessness into confidence?

....

....

....

....

....

What would your life look like if you viewed
yourself as a woman adored by God?

....

....

....

....

....

Given the choice of viewing life through the rose-colored glasses of hope rather than the dark blinders of sadness, anger, and worry, wouldn't it be far better to assume you'll find a foothold amid the chaos? After all, even if you go under, won't you have enjoyed the swim all the more if you sustain hope until the end rather than sinking into despair?

SUSAN VAUGHN

It is God that girdeth me with strength, and maketh my way perfect.

PSALM 18:32

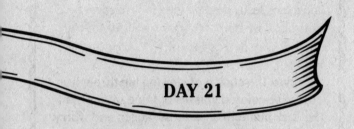

DAY 21

Knowing God

My people are destroyed
for lack of knowledge.
HOSEA 4:6

*A*s moms, it's our awesome responsibility to tell our children about the things of God. If we don't tell them about salvation, they'll never know that Jesus died on the cross to save them from sin. If we don't tell them about His unconditional love, they won't run to Him in times of trouble. If we don't tell them about healing, they'll never know that God can remedy their sicknesses. They need to know these important truths so that they won't perish for lack of knowledge.

Teaching our children God's Word and His ways are the two most important gifts we can give our kids, because if they have that knowledge, they have it all! As moms, we can't always be there for our children. But if we've equipped them with the knowledge of the Word of God, they will be all right without us, able to stand on their own.

It's like John Cougar Mellencamp says in one of his '80s tunes, "You've got to stand for something, or you're gonna fall for anything." If our children stand on the Word of God, they won't be easily fooled or swayed. So take the time to teach your children God's Word and ways. They are the most important investments you'll ever make.

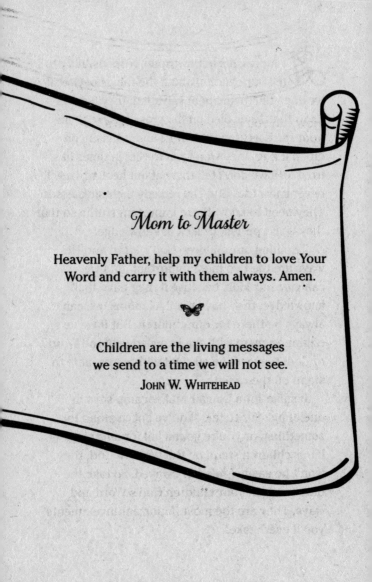

Mom to Master

Heavenly Father, help my children to love Your
Word and carry it with them always. Amen.

Children are the living messages
we send to a time we will not see.

JOHN W. WHITEHEAD

Think It Over

How can you instill in your children a love of God's Word?

....
....
....
....
....

What steps can you take to increase your and your children's knowledge of God's Word and ways?

....
....
....
....
....

How can you exemplify your unwavering dependence on scripture?

....
....
....
....
....

The Bible presents true truth, truth that is unchanging, truth that fits in with what exists, truth that answers the questions of life.

EDITH SCHAEFFER

So shall my word be that goeth forth out of my mouth: it shall not return unto me void, but it shall accomplish that which I please, and it shall prosper in the thing whereto I sent it.

ISAIAH 55:11

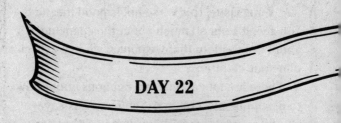

DAY 22

The Discipline of God

The rod and reproof give wisdom:
but a child left to himself bringeth
his mother to shame.

PROVERBS 29:15

No matter where you stand on the spanking issue, this verse holds good meaning. You see, it's not so much about the spanking, it's about the wisdom that we impart when we discipline our children.

There are lots of differing opinions about how to discipline our children. Some experts say we should spank them with our hands. Others say we should spank, but only with a paddle. Still others say we should never spank, only punish by other means. It seems there is a new theory every year. So what is the answer?

God is the only true answer. You must seek His face and ask His direction. He will teach you how to discipline your kids. He loves them even more than you do. He won't lead you astray. Just trust Him. Don't get caught up asking lots of people how you should discipline your kids. If you ask a hundred people, you'll get a hundred different perspectives. They don't know any more than you do. Go to the Source. He will impart wisdom to you so that you can impart wisdom to your children. You see, discipline and wisdom go hand in hand.

Mom to Master

Lord, teach me the best way
to discipline my children. Amen.

Some are kissing mothers and some are
scolding mothers, but it is love just the same—
and most mothers kiss and scold together.

PEARL S. BUCK

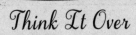

Think It Over

In what ways were you disciplined as a child?

....
....
....
....
....

How do you discipline your child(ren) today?

....
....
....
....
....

After disciplining your child, how do you reaffirm your love for him or her?

....
....
....
....
....

A God who had no love for me would
allow me to sin myself into oblivion.
In the same way, letting my child run
amok is not love. It is irresponsible.

CHRISTINE M. FIELD

Thou shalt also consider in thine heart,
that, as a man chasteneth his son,
so the LORD thy God chasteneth thee.

DEUTERONOMY 8:5

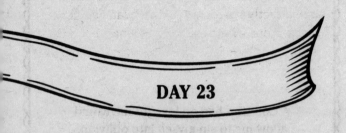

DAY 23

Don't Push My Buttons!

Thus will I bless thee while I live.

PSALM 63:4

*H*ave you ever watched members of a college cheerleading squad? Their motions are perfectly timed, in sync, on beat, and very sharp. If one member is behind a half a count, you'll be able to tell. Even minor flaws and mistakes are greatly magnified when the rest of the team is so good.

Do you ever feel like that cheerleader who is a half step behind the entire routine? Does it sometimes seem as if all the other moms have it all together, and you're kicking with the wrong leg? The devil loves to point out our shortcomings and whisper things like, "Hey, you are the worst mother ever. If you were a better mom, your children would be doing better in school."

See, the devil knows what buttons to push in order to make you feel the very worst—but don't let him have access to your buttons. When you start to compare yourself with another mother, stop yourself. Right then, begin thanking God for giving you the wisdom and strength to be the best mom you can be. When you respond to the devil's button-pushing with praise for God the Father, you will send the father of lies packing.

Mom to Master

Father, help me to be the best mom that
I can be. Help me to stop comparing
myself with others. I praise You. Amen.

What a relief to simply let go of my need to
do everything perfectly—and instead just do
everything for You! You know I'll always make
mistakes; You know that sometimes my best efforts
will look like failures to everybody else. Thank
You that I can simply relax and trust You to work
everything out according to Your plan.

DARLENE SALA

Think It Over

In what ways do you think you fall short as a mother?

....
....
....
....
....

Where does that message come from?

....
....
....
....
....

What Bible verses can you memorize to shore up your faith in God, His plan for you, and your mothering skills?

....
....
....
....
....

Each of us is divinely chosen to be the
mother of each child under our care.

ELISA MORGAN

*Let every man prove his own work,
and then shall he have rejoicing in
himself alone, and not in another.*

GALATIANS 6:4

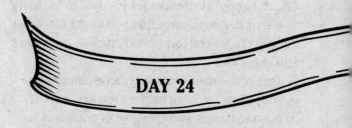

DAY 24

True Happiness

Give, and it shall be given unto you;
good measure, pressed down,
and shaken together, and running over.
LUKE 6:38

*D*id you know that God wants you to be happy? He desires for you to live life to its fullest. It doesn't matter that you might be elbow-deep in diapers or carpools right now—you can still enjoy life!

One of the main ways you can guarantee joy in your life is by living to give. You see, true happiness comes when we give of ourselves to others—our spouses, our children, our extended family, our church, our community, and our friends. As moms, we're sort of trained to be givers. We give up our careers, many times, to become full-time moms. We give up a full night's sleep to feed our babies. We give up sports cars for minivans and SUVs to accommodate our families. In fact, we'd give our lives for our children.

But sometimes our attitudes are less than joyful in all of our giving, right? Well, rejoice today. God promises to multiply back to you everything that you give. When you step out in faith, you open a door for God to move on your behalf. It's the simple principle of sowing and reaping. And as mothers, we are super sowers. So get ready for a super huge harvest!

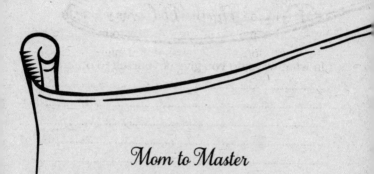

Mom to Master

Lord, help me to live to give with
the right attitude. I thank You. Amen.

Those who bring sunshine into the lives
of others cannot keep it from themselves.

JAMES M. BARRIE

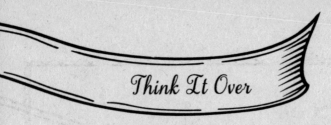

Think It Over

In what ways do you give of yourself to others?

....
....
....
....
....

How do you nurture yourself in the midst of all your giving?

....
....
....
....
....

What are some examples of God having multiplied back what you have given away?

....
....
....
....
....

Beyond giving of our material possessions,
God calls upon us to give our selves
away—our time, energy, and passion.

JILL BRISCOE

*Bring ye all the tithes into the storehouse,
that there may be meat in mine house,
and prove me now herewith, saith the LORD
of hosts, if I will not open you the windows of
heaven, and pour you out a blessing, that there
shall not be room enough to receive it.*

MALACHI 3:10

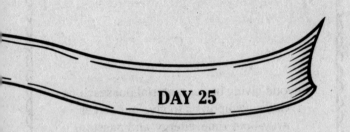

DAY 25

Letting Go

✎

*To him will I give the land that he hath
trodden upon, and to his children, because
he hath wholly followed the LORD.*

DEUTERONOMY 1:36

$\mathcal{H}$ave you ever heard the expression, "Let go and let God"? It's easier said than done. We sing songs in church about giving our all to God, such as "I Surrender All," when all the while, we're holding something back. How many times have we gone before God and asked Him to take over every part of our life, only later to have the Holy Spirit point out an area of our heart that we didn't give to God?

It's silly, isn't it? Why would we ever want to hold out on God? He doesn't want us to give our all so that He can make us miserable. He wants us to give our all so that He can bless us beyond our wildest dreams. God isn't some big ogre in the sky, just waiting for us to give our all to Him so that He can control us like puppets. He simply wants us to give our all so that we can walk in the plan that He has laid out for us. So if you're struggling with giving your all today, ask God to help you. Go ahead—let go and let God. He will give you much more in return.

Mom to Master

Lord, I give my all to You today. Help me
to leave my life in Your hands. Amen.

I wish for you the joy of holding life with an
open hand. Just let go of all the stuff you've had
to worry about and hang on to and protect. . . .
It isn't what you have that determines your
strength now or in the future. It is what you are
willing to let go of that is the ultimate test.

BOB BENSON

Think It Over

What, if anything, do you think you are holding
back from God?

....
....
....
....
....

In what ways can you pry your fingers loose in
order to give *all* to God?

....
....
....
....
....

What does it feel like to give God your whole
heart, mind, body, spirit, and soul?

....
....
....
....
....

If you try to surrender just a little bit to God, He'll know. It's like trying to carry on a conversation with someone who's preoccupied with the newspaper: most unsatisfying and practically useless.

KARON PHILLIPS GOODMAN

I beseech you therefore, brethren, by the mercies of God, that ye present your bodies a living sacrifice, holy, acceptable unto God, which is your reasonable service.

ROMANS 12:1

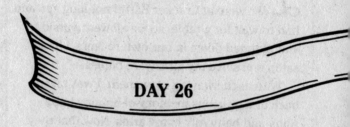

DAY 26

Rock. . .and Rest

He will not suffer thy foot to be moved:
he that keepeth thee will not slumber.

PSALM 121:3

I think the world needs more rocking chairs. We were at Cracker Barrel not long ago and had to wait for a table, so we all went outside and plopped down in our own rockers. I hadn't sat in one since my girls were babies.

With each swaying movement, I was taken back to a precious memory of holding baby Abby and baby Ally in my arms. Now that they are older, they don't sit on my lap very often. They are far "too cool" for that. Sometimes, I long for those rocking-chair days. Rockers force you to slow down and enjoy the moment. It's almost impossible to be stressed out while rocking. Sitting in a rocking chair is like cozying up to a close, old friend. There's something very comforting and comfortable about spending time in a rocker.

You know, even if you don't have a rocking chair at your house, you can spend some quality rocking time in God's rocker. When I pray to the Father, I always picture Him sitting in a big, wooden rocking chair and beckoning me to sit on His lap. If you need to de-stress today, crawl into your heavenly Father's lap and rock awhile.

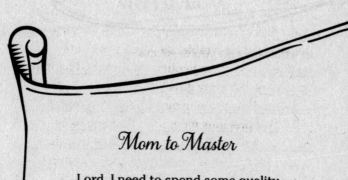

Mom to Master

Lord, I need to spend some quality
time just rocking with You today.
Thanks for loving me. Amen.

Jesus knows we must come apart and rest
awhile, or else we may just plain come apart.

Vance Havner

Think It Over

In what ways do you de-stress?

....
....
....
....
....

As you settle down to rest in the Lord, what methods do you use to calm your heart and mind?

....
....
....
....
....

What can you do to enjoy the moment in the middle of a harried day?

....
....
....
....
....

The Bible commands us to rest. . .
what a generous and kind God we have.
We expect marching orders, or hoops
to jump through. But God simply says,
"All right, this will be challenging, but here's
what I want you to do: take a break."

KERI WYATT KENT

*The LORD is my shepherd; I shall
not want. He maketh me to lie down
in green pastures: he leadeth me beside
the still waters. He restoreth my soul.*

PSALM 23:1–3

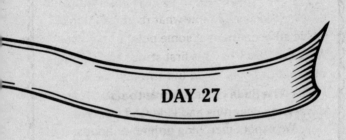

DAY 27

Just What You Need

*Your Father knoweth what things
ye have need of, before ye ask him.*

MATTHEW 6:8

$\mathcal{H}$ave you ever been so distraught that you didn't even know what to pray? I think we've all been there at some point in our lives. After my father had his first stroke and they didn't know if he would live through the night, I became numb. It was touch and go for several days, and all I did was drive to and from the hospital. On those forty-minute drives, I would try to pray, but all I could do was say the name of Jesus. Thankfully, that was enough.

In Matthew 6:8, the Word tells us that God knows what we need even before we ask Him. That's good to know, isn't it? Even when we can't pray what we want to pray, God knows our hearts. He knows what we need. If we simply call on the name of Jesus, He is right there beside us.

No matter how desperate you are today, no matter how hopeless you feel, no matter how far from God you think you are. . .God loves you. He wants to help you. He wants to help your children. He wants to bring you through this difficult time. Call on Him today.

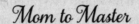

Mom to Master

Thank You, Lord, for knowing me so
well and hearing my heart. Amen.

What seem our worst prayers may really be,
in God's eyes, our best. Those, I mean, which are
least supported by devotional feeling. For these
may come from a deeper level than feeling. God
sometimes seems to speak to us most intimately
when He catches us, as it were, off our guard.

C. S. LEWIS

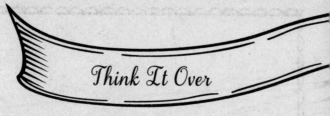

Think It Over

At what times have you only been able to cry out, "Jesus, help!"?

....

....

....

....

How does it make you feel knowing that God understands the meaning of your groans in the same way you understand the cries of your children?

....

....

....

....

How would your faith increase if you focused on the reality that "our worst prayers may really be, in God's eyes, our best"?

....

....

....

....

True prayer is measured by weight,
not by length. A single groan before
God may have more fullness of prayer in
it than a fine oration of great length.

CHARLES SPURGEON

Likewise the Spirit also helpeth our infirmities:
for we know not what we should pray for as we
ought: but the Spirit itself maketh intercession for
us with groanings which cannot be uttered.

ROMANS 8:26

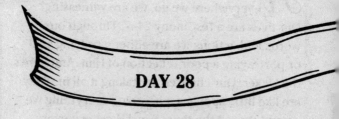

DAY 28

Parrot-hood

It were better for him that a millstone were hanged about his neck, and he cast into the sea, than that he should offend one of these little ones.

LUKE 17:2

*H*ow is your witness? Do you know that everywhere we go, we are witnessing? Our lives are a testimony 24–7. Through our words and actions we are either glorifying God or portraying a poor reflection of Him. And here's the kicker: Our children are taking it all in. They are like little sponges, absorbing everything we do and say, all the time. Wow! Have you ever thought about that reality? Our kids may be basing their view of Christianity on how we behave. Oh my!

I first realized that fact when my daughter Abby was just a toddler. She was a miniature parrot. She repeated absolutely everything I said—good or bad. Once I was on the phone with my mother, and I said that someone had acted like a horse's behind. Later that night when Allyson drooled on one of Abby's favorite dolls, Abby said, "You are a horse's behind!" While it was funny, it was sad, too. I knew exactly where she had heard the expression—from me!

So like the song says, "Be careful, little mouth, what you say," and go forth and give a good witness. You have an attentive audience nearby.

Mom to Master

Lord, help me to be a good reflection
of You all the time. Help me to point
my children toward You. Amen.

Most of the people who will walk after
me will be children, so make the beat
keep time with short steps.

HANS CHRISTIAN ANDERSEN

Think It Over

In what ways do you see your children mimicking your words and actions?

....
....
....
....
....

Is this a true reflection of God?

....
....
....
....
....

What can you do to remind yourself you may be the only Bible some people ever read—and act accordingly?

....
....
....
....
....

In my teens, I was approached by a total stranger on a crowded city street. She said, "You are Kae Cameron's daughter, I'd recognize her face anywhere!" And she was right. How I long for the day when people look at my life and say. "Oh, you must be a daughter of the heavenly Father, I recognize His face anywhere!"

KATHERINE WALDEN

Christ. . .[left] us an example,
that ye should follow his steps.

1 PETER 2:21

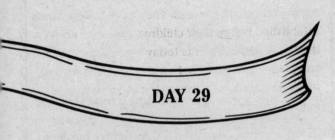

DAY 29

Real Growth

But Jesus said, Suffer little children,
and forbid them not, to come unto me:
for of such is the kingdom of heaven.

MATTHEW 19:14

Parents today are quite proactive. They have their unborn babies on waiting lists for the top preschools in the area. They have college funds established before their children have ever spoken their first words. Parents today are really thinking and planning ahead. That's a good thing; however, many parents are neglecting the most crucial part of their children's lives—their salvation.

While it's wonderful to put so much thought into the proper preschool for our little ones, it's much more important to make sure we're attending a church that will nurture and encourage our children's spiritual development. If you're in a church that doesn't have a strong children's ministry—one that simply entertains and baby-sits the kids—seek God's guidance. It may be time to either consider volunteering your time to help improve the present ministry or to seek a new place of worship. Let's face it, being good dodgeball players isn't going to help our children when they are facing peer pressure. They need a church that will keep them grounded in the Word no matter what life brings to them. Let's be proactive about our children's spiritual lives. There's nothing more important.

Mom to Master

Lord, please give me direction in regard to
helping my children get the best spiritual
education in a church. Amen.

There are only two lasting bequests
we can hope to give our children.
One is roots; the other, wings.

HODDING CARTER

Think It Over

How well does your church minister to and educate your children spiritually?

....

....

....

....

....

In what ways do you help *all* children become stronger in the church and in the Lord?

....

....

....

....

....

What areas could you contribute to in order to make your church's children's program better?

....

....

....

....

....

Churches are in the business of
creating a new heaven and a new
earth, not satisfying shareholders.

BRAD BERGLUND

*Train up a child in the way he should go:
and when he is old, he will not depart from it.*

PROVERBS 22:6

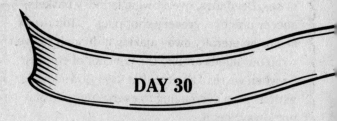

DAY 30

Momentary Meditation

But the mercy of the Lord is from everlasting
to everlasting upon them that fear him.

Psalm 103:17

$\mathcal{L}$ ife is just so busy! There are some days when we can't see past the end of our noses. Deadlines, overflowing laundry baskets, soccer practice, grocery shopping. . . Tomorrow seems an eternity away making it difficult to even wrap our minds around the concept of eternity. So when we read a verse that says God's love is with us from everlasting to everlasting, we may not always get it.

During your Bible study time, ask God to turn off the to-do list part of your brain so that you can really hear God's voice through His Word. It really works! Suddenly, His Word leaps off the page, and all at once, you'll get it!

Psalm 103:17 is an awesome go-to verse when you want to grasp the awesomeness of God and His adoration of you. To think that someone—especially the Creator of the universe—could love you forever and ever is so great! What a wonderful promise!

As moms we don't have a lot of time to meditate on God's Word, so we have to make the most of those moments with the Master. Ask God to help you really focus as you read the Bible. Ask Him to show you what He has especially for you each day. It's exciting!

Mom to Master

Lord, help me to meditate
more on Your Word. Amen.

In the noise and clatter of my kitchen. . .
I possess God in as great tranquility
as if I were on my knees.

BROTHER LAWRENCE

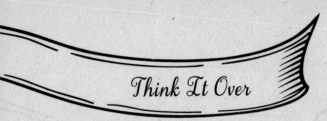

Think It Over

What is keeping you, if anything, from hearing God speak to you from His Word?

....
....
....
....
....

What are some favorite Bible verses that can help you get into the God mind-set?

....
....
....
....
....

How can you improve your quality time with God?

....
....
....
....
....

Meditation teaches us to become like tea bags, soaking deeply and quietly in God and His Word so that we can better hear him speak to our hearts and minds.

VALERIE HESS AND MARTI WATSON GARLETT

Meditate upon these things; give thyself wholly to them; that thy profiting may appear to all.

1 TIMOTHY 4:15

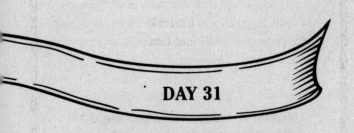

DAY 31

Spiritual Fruitcake

*But the fruit of the Spirit is love, joy,
peace, longsuffering, gentleness,
goodness, faith, meekness, temperance.*
GALATIANS 5:22–23

$\mathcal{D}$id you receive a fruit basket last Christmas? How about a fruitcake? Perhaps you like fruit baskets and fruitcake or enjoy giving them to your friends and family members during certain times of the year.

But there's something even better than giving a fruity gift—it's giving the fruit of the Spirit. It's one of the best gifts to give to or bless those around us. But we don't have to just give such fruit only during the holidays—we can radiate those qualities year-round!

Our children need to see us exuding those characteristics. They need to feel that love, joy, peace, patience, kindness, goodness, faithfulness, gentleness, and self-control operating in our homes. Sure, we're going to miss the mark once in a while, but as long as we're growing in those attributes and, when necessary, apologizing to our kids for falling short, that's all that counts. God isn't keeping score on how many times we lose self-control; rather, He is celebrating with us as we grow in every fruit. So, go on. Give good fruit today!

Mom to Master

Thank You, God, for the fruit of the Spirit.
Help me to grow in each fruit so that
I'll become more like You. Amen.

Joy is love exalted, peace is love in repose;
long-suffering is love enduring; gentleness is
love in society; goodness is love in action;
faith is love on the battlefield; meekness is love
in school; and temperance is love in training.

D. L. MOODY

Think It Over

What fruit(s) of the Spirit do you find challenging to attain?

....
....
....
....
....

What fruit(s) of the Spirit do you currently exemplify to your children?

....
....
....
....
....

In what ways can you hone your "walk in the Spirit" (Galatians 5:25) so that you'll reap a bountiful harvest?

....
....
....
....
....

Leaves and flowers and fruit must surely come in
their season; for your Husbandman is skillful,
and He never fails in His harvesting.

HANNAH WHITALL SMITH

The divine Husbandsman who has the care of the
Vine will care also for you who are His brances
and will so prune and purge and water and tend
you that you will grow and bring forth fruit,
and your fruit shall remain, and, like the lily,
you shall find yourself arryed in apparel so
glorious that of Solomon will be as nothing to it.

HANNAH WHITALL SMITH

*I am the vine, ye are the branches: He that abideth
in me, and I in him, the same bringeth forth
much fruit: for without me ye can do nothing.*

JOHN 15:5